THE APOLOGY TO NATIVE HAWAIIANS

on behalf of the United States
for the
Overthrow of the Kingdom of Hawaii

Introduction by Richard J. Scudder

Ka'imi Pono Press
a division of Blue-Green Delta Ltd.

A complete reprint of the U.S. Congress Public Law 103-150 and the U.S. Senate Committee on Indian Affairs Report 109-126, originally printed by the U.S. Government Printing Office.

Introduction by Richard J. Scudder

All rights reserved.

Cover design, and introduction Copyright © 1994 by Kaʻimi Pono Press, a division of Blue-Green Delta Ltd.

Printed by Valenti Brothers Graphics, Honolulu.

Library of Congress Cataloging-in-Publication Data

The Apology to Native Hawaiians
U.S. Congress, (reprinted)
with an introduction by Richard J. Scudder.
ISBN 0-9643829-0-3 5.95

   1. History-Hawaii
   2. U.S. Congress
   3. Native Hawaiians
   4. Scudder, Richard J.

I. Title

Kaʻimi Pono Press
a division of Blue-Green Delta Ltd.
91-216 Holoimua Place
Kapolei, HI 96707

10 9 8 7 6 5 4 3 2

Contents

Title *1*
Publishing Information *2*
Contents *3*
Introduction *5*

PART 1
Public Law 103-150, Nov. 23, 1993, 103d Congress, S.J. Res. 19 .... *(1510)*
Joint Resolution, To Acknowledge the 100th Anniversary of the
January 17, 1893 Overthrow of the Kingdom of Hawaii, and to Offer
an Apology to Native Hawaiians on Behalf of the United States for
the Overthrow of the Kingdom of Hawaii.
    Findings
    Resolves
    Sec. 1. Acknowledgement and Apology .... *(1513)*
    Sec. 2. Definitions .... *(1513)*
    Sec. 3. Disclaimer .... *(1514)*
    Approval Date .... *(1514)*
    Signatures: .... *(1514)*
        Speaker of the House
        President of the Senate pro tempore
        President of the United States
    Legislative History .... *(1514)*

PART 2
Senate Committee on Indian Affairs Report 109-126 .... *(1)*
    Purpose .... *(1)*
    Background .... *(2)*
        Treaties and Other International Agreements of
        the United States of America 1776-1949
    Hawaiian Islands Commerce 1826 .... *(2)*
    A Compilation of the Messages and Papers of the Presidents 1789-1902 ...... *(4)*
    Friendship, Commerce and Navigation 1849 .... *(7)*
    Commercial Reciprocity 1875 .... *(15)*
    The Statutes at large of the United States of America, ... *(19)*
        from December 1887 to March 1889, and Recent Treaties,
        Postal Conventions, and Executive Proclamations
    By the President of the United States, ... *(19)*
        A Proclamation 1887
    The Overthrow (summary) .... *(21)*
        President's Message (to Congress) Relating to the
        Hawaiian Islands–December 18, 1893
    Annexation to Statehood (summary) .... *(34)*
    Legislative History .... *(34)*
    Committee Recommendation and Tabulation of Vote .... *(34)*
    Section-by-Section Analysis .... *(34)*
    Regulatory Impact Statement .... *(35)*
    Executive Communications .... *(35)*
    Changes in Existing Law .... *(35)*
Resolution *47*
Order Information *48*

INTRODUCTION

The Ka'imi Pono Press believes that the full text of the Apology to Native Hawaiians on Behalf of the United States for the Overthrow of the Kingdom of Hawaii, and the supporting materials found in the Report of the Senate Committee on Indian Affairs should be widely available.

Included in the Committee Report is President Grover Cleveland's Message to Congress of December 12, 1893, where he writes, "By an act of war, committed with the participation of a diplomatic representative of the United States and without authority of Congress, the Government of a feeble but friendly and confiding people has been overthrown. A substantial wrong has thus been done which a due regard for our national character as well as the rights of the injured people requires we should endeavor to repair."

It took one hundred years, but the first step, the apology to Native Hawaiians has been given. The time has come for reconciliation efforts between the United States and Native Hawaiians, as recognized in the resolution and the acknowledgement by President William Clinton.

The Ka'imi Pono Press acknowledges the efforts of Senator's Daniel K. Inouye and Daniel K. Akaka in obtaining the acknowledgement of the overthrow, the apology, the recognition of the need for reconciliation between the United States and Native Hawaiians, and the need by the United States of America to address the rights of Native Hawaiians to self-determination.

The Ka'imi Pono Press also commends President William Clinton in his acknowledging the ramifications of the overthrow of the Kingdom of Hawaii and to supporting reconciliation efforts between the United States and the Native Hawaiian people.

-Richard J. Scudder

PUBLIC LAW 103-150—NOV. 23, 1993

100TH ANNIVERSARY OF THE OVERTHROW OF THE HAWAIIAN KINGDOM

S. J. Res. 19

PUBLIC LAW 103-150

One Hundred Third Congress
of the
United States of America

AT THE FIRST SESSION

Begun and held at the City of Washington on Tuesday, the fifth day of January, one thousand nine hundred and ninety-three

Joint Resolution

107 STAT. 1510　　PUBLIC LAW 103-150—NOV. 23, 1993

Public Law 103-150
103d Congress

Joint Resolution

Nov. 23, 1993
[S.J. Res. 19]

To acknowledge the 100th anniversary of the January 17, 1893 overthrow of the Kingdom of Hawaii, and to offer an apology to Native Hawaiians on behalf of the United States for the overthrow of the Kingdom of Hawaii.

Whereas, prior to the arrival of the first Europeans in 1778, the Native Hawaiian people lived in a highly organized, self-sufficient, subsistent social system based on communal land tenure with a sophisticated language, culture, and religion;

Whereas a unified monarchical government of the Hawaiian Islands was established in 1810 under Kamehameha I, the first King of Hawaii;

Whereas, from 1826 until 1893, the United States recognized the independence of the Kingdom of Hawaii, extended full and complete diplomatic recognition to the Hawaiian Government, and entered into treaties and conventions with the Hawaiian monarchs to govern commerce and navigation in 1826, 1842, 1849, 1875, and 1887;

Whereas the Congregational Church (now known as the United Church of Christ), through its American Board of Commissioners for Foreign Missions, sponsored and sent more than 100 missionaries to the Kingdom of Hawaii between 1820 and 1850;

Whereas, on January 14, 1893, John L. Stevens (hereafter referred to in this Resolution as the "United States Minister"), the United States Minister assigned to the sovereign and independent Kingdom of Hawaii conspired with a small group of non-Hawaiian residents of the Kingdom of Hawaii, including citizens of the United States, to overthrow the indigenous and lawful Government of Hawaii;

Whereas, in pursuance of the conspiracy to overthrow the Government of Hawaii, the United States Minister and the naval representatives of the United States caused armed naval forces of the United States to invade the sovereign Hawaiian nation on January 16, 1893, and to position themselves near the Hawaiian Government buildings and the Iolani Palace to intimidate Queen Liliuokalani and her Government;

Whereas, on the afternoon of January 17, 1893, a Committee of Safety that represented the American and European sugar planters, descendents of missionaries, and financiers deposed the Hawaiian monarchy and proclaimed the establishment of a Provisional Government;

Whereas the United States Minister thereupon extended diplomatic recognition to the Provisional Government that was formed by the conspirators without the consent of the Native Hawaiian

people or the lawful Government of Hawaii and in violation of treaties between the two nations and of international law;
Whereas, soon thereafter, when informed of the risk of bloodshed with resistance, Queen Liliuokalani issued the following statement yielding her authority to the United States Government rather than to the Provisional Government:

"I Liliuokalani, by the Grace of God and under the Constitution of the Hawaiian Kingdom, Queen, do hereby solemnly protest against any and all acts done against myself and the Constitutional Government of the Hawaiian Kingdom by certain persons claiming to have established a Provisional Government of and for this Kingdom.

"That I yield to the superior force of the United States of America whose Minister Plenipotentiary, His Excellency John L. Stevens, has caused United States troops to be landed at Honolulu and declared that he would support the Provisional Government.

"Now to avoid any collision of armed forces, and perhaps the loss of life, I do this under protest and impelled by said force yield my authority until such time as the Government of the United States shall, upon facts being presented to it, undo the action of its representatives and reinstate me in the authority which I claim as the Constitutional Sovereign of the Hawaiian Islands.".

Done at Honolulu this 17th day of January, A.D. 1893.;
Whereas, without the active support and intervention by the United States diplomatic and military representatives, the insurrection against the Government of Queen Liliuokalani would have failed for lack of popular support and insufficient arms;
Whereas, on February 1, 1893, the United States Minister raised the American flag and proclaimed Hawaii to be a protectorate of the United States;
Whereas the report of a Presidentially established investigation conducted by former Congressman James Blount into the events surrounding the insurrection and overthrow of January 17, 1893, concluded that the United States diplomatic and military representatives had abused their authority and were responsible for the change in government;
Whereas, as a result of this investigation, the United States Minister to Hawaii was recalled from his diplomatic post and the military commander of the United States armed forces stationed in Hawaii was disciplined and forced to resign his commission;
Whereas, in a message to Congress on December 18, 1893, President Grover Cleveland reported fully and accurately on the illegal acts of the conspirators, described such acts as an "act of war, committed with the participation of a diplomatic representative of the United States and without authority of Congress", and acknowledged that by such acts the government of a peaceful and friendly people was overthrown;
Whereas President Cleveland further concluded that a "substantial wrong has thus been done which a due regard for our national character as well as the rights of the injured people requires we should endeavor to repair" and called for the restoration of the Hawaiian monarchy;
Whereas the Provisional Government protested President Cleveland's call for the restoration of the monarchy and continued to hold state power and pursue annexation to the United States;
Whereas the Provisional Government successfully lobbied the Committee on Foreign Relations of the Senate (hereafter referred

to in this Resolution as the "Committee") to conduct a new investigation into the events surrounding the overthrow of the monarchy;

Whereas the Committee and its chairman, Senator John Morgan, conducted hearings in Washington, D.C., from December 27, 1893, through February 26, 1894, in which members of the Provisional Government justified and condoned the actions of the United States Minister and recommended annexation of Hawaii;

Whereas, although the Provisional Government was able to obscure the role of the United States in the illegal overthrow of the Hawaiian monarchy, it was unable to rally the support from two-thirds of the Senate needed to ratify a treaty of annexation;

Whereas, on July 4, 1894, the Provisional Government declared itself to be the Republic of Hawaii;

Whereas, on January 24, 1895, while imprisoned in Iolani Palace, Queen Liliuokalani was forced by representatives of the Republic of Hawaii to officially abdicate her throne;

Whereas, in the 1896 United States Presidential election, William McKinley replaced Grover Cleveland;

Whereas, on July 7, 1898, as a consequence of the Spanish-American War, President McKinley signed the Newlands Joint Resolution that provided for the annexation of Hawaii;

Whereas, through the Newlands Resolution, the self-declared Republic of Hawaii ceded sovereignty over the Hawaiian Islands to the United States;

Whereas the Republic of Hawaii also ceded 1,800,000 acres of crown, government and public lands of the Kingdom of Hawaii, without the consent of or compensation to the Native Hawaiian people of Hawaii or their sovereign government;

Whereas the Congress, through the Newlands Resolution, ratified the cession, annexed Hawaii as part of the United States, and vested title to the lands in Hawaii in the United States;

Whereas the Newlands Resolution also specified that treaties existing between Hawaii and foreign nations were to immediately cease and be replaced by United States treaties with such nations;

Whereas the Newlands Resolution effected the transaction between the Republic of Hawaii and the United States Government;

Whereas the indigenous Hawaiian people never directly relinquished their claims to their inherent sovereignty as a people or over their national lands to the United States, either through their monarchy or through a plebiscite or referendum;

Whereas, on April 30, 1900, President McKinley signed the Organic Act that provided a government for the territory of Hawaii and defined the political structure and powers of the newly established Territorial Government and its relationship to the United States;

Whereas, on August 21, 1959, Hawaii became the 50th State of the United States;

Whereas the health and well-being of the Native Hawaiian people is intrinsically tied to their deep feelings and attachment to the land;

Whereas the long-range economic and social changes in Hawaii over the nineteenth and early twentieth centuries have been devastating to the population and to the health and well-being of the Hawaiian people;

Whereas the Native Hawaiian people are determined to preserve, develop and transmit to future generations their ancestral territory, and their cultural identity in accordance with their own spiritual and traditional beliefs, customs, practices, language, and social institutions;

Whereas, in order to promote racial harmony and cultural understanding, the Legislature of the State of Hawaii has determined that the year 1993 should serve Hawaii as a year of special reflection on the rights and dignities of the Native Hawaiians in the Hawaiian and the American societies;

Whereas the Eighteenth General Synod of the United Church of Christ in recognition of the denomination's historical complicity in the illegal overthrow of the Kingdom of Hawaii in 1893 directed the Office of the President of the United Church of Christ to offer a public apology to the Native Hawaiian people and to initiate the process of reconciliation between the United Church of Christ and the Native Hawaiians; and

Whereas it is proper and timely for the Congress on the occasion of the impending one hundredth anniversary of the event, to acknowledge the historic significance of the illegal overthrow of the Kingdom of Hawaii, to express its deep regret to the Native Hawaiian people, and to support the reconciliation efforts of the State of Hawaii and the United Church of Christ with Native Hawaiians: Now, therefore, be it

Resolved by the Senate and House of Representatives of the United States of America in Congress assembled,

SECTION 1. ACKNOWLEDGMENT AND APOLOGY.

The Congress—

(1) on the occasion of the 100th anniversary of the illegal overthrow of the Kingdom of Hawaii on January 17, 1893, acknowledges the historical significance of this event which resulted in the suppression of the inherent sovereignty of the Native Hawaiian people;

(2) recognizes and commends efforts of reconciliation initiated by the State of Hawaii and the United Church of Christ with Native Hawaiians;

(3) apologizes to Native Hawaiians on behalf of the people of the United States for the overthrow of the Kingdom of Hawaii on January 17, 1893 with the participation of agents and citizens of the United States, and the deprivation of the rights of Native Hawaiians to self-determination;

(4) expresses its commitment to acknowledge the ramifications of the overthrow of the Kingdom of Hawaii, in order to provide a proper foundation for reconciliation between the United States and the Native Hawaiian people; and

(5) urges the President of the United States to also acknowledge the ramifications of the overthrow of the Kingdom of Hawaii and to support reconciliation efforts between the United States and the Native Hawaiian people.

SEC. 2. DEFINITIONS.

As used in this Joint Resolution, the term "Native Hawaiian" means any individual who is a descendent of the aboriginal people who, prior to 1778, occupied and exercised sovereignty in the area that now constitutes the State of Hawaii.

SEC. 3. DISCLAIMER.

Nothing in this Joint Resolution is intended to serve as a settlement of any claims against the United States.

Approved November 23, 1993.

Speaker of the House of Representatives.

~~Vice President of the United States and~~ *President of the Senate pro tempore.*

APPROVED
NOV 23 1993

LEGISLATIVE HISTORY—S.J. Res. 19:

SENATE REPORTS: No. 103-126 (Select Comm. on Indian Affairs).
CONGRESSIONAL RECORD, Vol. 139 (1993):
   Oct. 27, considered and passed Senate.
   Nov. 15, considered and passed House.

Calendar No. 185

103D CONGRESS			REPORT
1st Session		SENATE	103-126

ACKNOWLEDGING THE 100TH ANNIVERSARY OF THE JANUARY 17, 1893 OVERTHROW OF THE KINGDOM OF HAWAII, AND TO OFFER AN APOLOGY TO NATIVE HAWAIIANS ON BEHALF OF THE UNITED STATES FOR THE OVERTHROW OF THE KINGDOM OF HAWAII

AUGUST 6 (legislative day, JUNE 30), 1993.—Ordered to be printed

Mr. INOUYE, from the Committee on Indian Affairs, submitted the following

REPORT

[To accompany S.J. Res. 19]

The Committee on Indian Affairs, to which was referred the joint resolution (S.J. Res. 19) to acknowledge the 100th anniversary of the January 17, 1893 overthrow of the Kingdom of Hawaii, and to offer an apology to Native Hawaiians on behalf of the United States for the overthrow of the Kingdom of Hawaii, having considered the same, reports favorably thereon without amendment and recommends that the joint resolution do pass.

PURPOSE

S.J. Res. 19, to acknowledge the 100 anniversary of the January 17, 1893 overthrow of the Kingdom of Hawaii, and to offer an apology to Native Hawaiians on behalf of the United States for the overthrow of the Kingdom of Hawaii, was introduced by Senator Akaka (for himself and Senator Inouye) on January 21, 1993. The purpose of S.J. Res. 19 is to acknowledge the historical significance of the January 17, 1893 overthrow of the Kingdom of Hawaii on the occasion of the 100th anniversary of this event; to offer an apology to Native Hawaiians on behalf of the United States for the overthrow of the Kingdom of Hawaii, with the participation of citizens and agents of the United States; to commend efforts of reconciliation initiated by the State of Hawaii and the United Church of Christ with Native Hawaiians; and to urge reconciliation efforts between the United States and the Native Hawaiian people.

69-010

BACKGROUND

Following the first European contact with the Hawaiian Islands by British Captain James Cook in 1778, U.S. involvement with the Hawaiians Islands began in the early 19th century with the arrival of American missionaries and traders. By that time, a unified monarchial government was established under King Kamehameha I, the first King of Hawaii.

While American businessmen and missionaries increased their economic, social, and political influence in the Hawaiian Islands, the introduction of christianity had a significant impact on Native Hawaiian religion, culture and values. The Congregational Church (now known as the United Church of Christ), through its American Board of Commissioners for Foreign Missions, sponsored and sent the first missionaries to the Kingdom of Hawaii between 1820 and 1850.

In 1826, the Kingdom of Hawaii entered into its first international treaty with the United States. Although the treaty, which was intended to safeguard U.S. ships, was never ratified by the United States, it nevertheless served as a "treaty of friendship" between the United States and the Kingdom of Hawaii. Article I declared that peace and friendship between the United States and the Kingdom of Hawaii were "perpetual." Subsequent presidential messages, conventions, and treaties in 1842, 1849, 1875, and 1887, between the two nations or by the United States, extended U.S. diplomatic recognition to the Hawaiian government and affirmed U.S. recognition of the sovereignty and independence of the Hawaiian Kingdom. The documents are as follows:

TREATIES AND OTHER INTERNATIONAL AGREEMENTS OF THE UNITED STATES OF AMERICA 1776–1949

(Compiled under the direction of Charles I. Bevans, LL.B., Assistant Legal Adviser, Department of State)

HAWAIIAN ISLANDS

COMMERCE

Articles of arrangement signed at Honolulu December 23, 1826
Entered into force December 23, 1826
Apparently superseded in effect by treaty of December 20, 1849 [1]—3 Miller 269.
Articles of arrangement made and concluded at Oahu between Thomas ap Catesby Jones appointed by the United States, of the one part, and Kauileaouli, King of the Sandwich Islands, and his Guardians, on the other part.

Art: 1st

The peace and friendship subsisting between the United States, and their Majesties, the Queen Regent, and Kauikeaouli, King of the Sandwich Islands, and their sub-

---

[1] Post, p. 864.

jects and people, are hereby confirmed, and declared to be perpetual.

Art: 2nd

The ships and vessels of the United States (as well as their Consuls and all other citizens within the territorial jurisdiction of the Sandwich Islands, together with all their property), shall be inviolably protected against *all* Enemies of the United States in time of war.

Art: 3rd

The contracting parties being desirous to avail themselves of the bounties of Divine Providence, by promoting the commercial intercourse and friendship subsisting between the respective nations, for the better security of these desirable objects, Their Majesties bind themselves to receive into their Ports and Harbours all ships and vessels of the United States; and to protect, to the uttermost of their capacity, all such ships and vessels, their cargoes, officers and crews, so long as they shall behave themselves peacefully, and not infringe the established laws of the land, the citizens of the United States being permitted to trade freely with the people of the Sandwich Islands.

Art: 4th

Their Majesties do further agree to extend the fullest protection, within their control, to all ships and vessels of the United States which may be wrecked on their shores; and to render every assistance in their power to save the wreck and her apparel and cargo; and as a reward for the assistance and protection which the people of the Sandwich Islands shall afford to all such distressed vessels of the United States, they shall be entitled to a salvage, or a portion of the property so saved; but such salvage shall, in no case, exceed one third of the value saved; which valuation is to be fixed by a commission of disinterested persons who shall be chosen equally by the Parties.

Art: 5th

Citizens of the United States, whether resident or transient, engaged in commerce, or trading to the Sandwich Islands, shall be inviolably protected in their lawful pursuits; and shall be allowed to sue for, and recover, by judgment, all claims against the subjects of His Majesty The King, according to strict principles of equity, and the acknowledged practice of civilized nations.

Art: 6th

Their Majesties do further agree and bind themselves to discountenance and use all practicable means to prevent desertion from all American ships which visit the Sandwich Islands; and to that end it shall be made the duty of all Governors, Magistrates, Chiefs of Districts, and all others in authority, to apprehend all deserters; and to deliver them over to the master of the vessel from which they have deserted; and for the apprehension of every such deserter, who shall be delivered over as aforesaid, the master, owner, or agent, shall pay to the person or persons apprehending such deserter, the sum of six Dollars, if taken on the side of the Island near which the vessel is anchored; but if taken on the opposite side of the Island, the sum shall be twelve Dollars; and if taken on any other Island, the reward shall be twenty four Dollars, and shall be a just charge against the wages of every such deserter.

Art: 7th

No tonnage dues or impost shall be exacted of any Citizen of the United States which is not paid by the Citizens or subjects of the nation most favoured in commerce with the Sandwich Islands; and the citizens or subjects of the Sandwich Islands shall be allowed to trade with the United States, and her territories, upon principles of equal advantage with the most favoured nation.

Done in council at Honolulu, Island of Woahoo, this 23rd day of December in the year of our Lord 1826.

THOS. AP CATESBY JONES.
ELISABETA KAAHUMANU.
KARAIMOKU.
POKI.
HOWAPILI.
LIDIA NAMAHANA.

A COMPILATION OF THE MESSAGES AND PAPERS OF THE PRESIDENTS 1789–1902

(By James D. Richardson, A Representative from the State of Tennessee)

Washington, December 30, 1842.

To the Senate and House of Representatives of the United States:

I communicate herewith to Congress copies of a correspondence which has recently taken place between certain agents of the Government of the Hawaiian or Sandwich Islands and the Secretary of State.

The condition of those islands has excited a good deal of interest, which is increasing by every successive proof that their inhabitants are making progress in civilization and becoming more and more competent to maintain regular and orderly civil government. They lie in the Pacific Ocean, much nearer to this continent that the other, and have become an important place for the refitment and provisioning of American and European vessels.

Owing to their locality and to the course of the winds which prevail in this quarter of the world, the Sandwich Islands are the stopping place for almost all vessels passing from continent to continent across the Pacific Ocean. They are especially resorted to by the great number of vessels of the United States which are engaged in the whale fishery in those seas. The number of vessels of all sorts and the amount of property owned by citizens of the United States which are found in those islands in the course of the year are stated probably with sufficient accuracy in the letter of the agents.

Just emerging from a state of barbarism, the Government of the islands is as yet feeble, but its dispositions appear to be just and pacific, and it seems anxious to improve the condition of its people by the introduction of knowledge, of religious and moral institutions, means of education, and the arts of civilized life.

It can not but be in conformity with the interest and wishes of the Government and the people of the United States that this community, thus existing in the midst of a vast expanse of ocean, should be respected and all its rights strictly and conscientiously regarded; and this must also be the true interest of all commercial states. Far remote from the dominions of European powers, its growth and prosperity as an independent state may yet be in a high degree useful to all whose trade is extended to those regions; while its near approach to this continent and the intercourse which American vessels have with it, such vessels constituent five-sixths of all which annually visit it, could not but create dissatisfaction on the part of the United States at any attempt by another power, should such attempt be threatened or feared, to take possession of the islands, colonize them, and subvert the native Government. Considering, therefore, that the United States possesses so large a share of the intercourse with those islands, it is deemed not unfit to make the declaration that their Government seeks, nevertheless, no peculiar advantages, no exclusive control over the Hawaiian Government, but is content with its independent existence and anxiously wishes for its security and prosperity. Its forbearance in this respect under the circumstances of the very large intercourse of their citizens with the islands would justify this Government, should events hereafter arise to require it, in making a decided remonstrance against the adoption of an opposite policy by any other power. Under the circumstances I recommend to Congress to provide for a moderate allowance to be made out of the Treasury to the consul residing there, that in a Government so new and a country so remote American citizens may have respectable authority to which to apply for redress in case of injury to their persons and property, and to whom the Government of the country may also make known any acts committed by American citizens of which it may think it has a right to complain.

Events of considerable importance have recently transpired in China. The military operations carried on against that Empire by the English Government have been terminated by a treaty, according to the terms of which four important ports hitherto shut against foreign commerce are to be open to British merchants, viz, Amoy, Foo-Choo-Foo,

Ningpo, and Chinghai. It can not but be interesting to the mercantile interest of the United States, whose intercourse with China at the single port of Canton has already become so considerable, to ascertain whether these other ports now open to British commerce are to remain shut, nevertheless, against the commerce of the United States. The treaty between the Chinese Government and the British commissioner provides neither for the admission nor the exclusion of the ships of other nations. It would seem, therefore, that it remains with every other nation having commercial intercourse with China to seek to make proper arrangements for itself with the Government of that Empire in this respect.

The importations into the United States from China are known to be large, having amounted in some years, as will be seen by the annexed tables, to $9,000,000. The exports, too, from the United States to China constitute an interesting and growing part of the commerce of the country. It appears that in the year 1841, in the direct trade between the two countries, the value of the exports from the United States amounted to $715,000 in domestic produce and $485,000 in foreign merchandise. But the whole amount of American produce which finally reaches China and is there consumed is not comprised in these tables, which show only the direct trade. Many vessels with American products on board sail with a primary destination to other countries, but ultimately dispose of more or less of their cargoes in the port of Canton.

The peculiarities of the Chinese Government and the Chinese character are well known. An Empire supposed to contain 300,000,000 subjects, fertile in various rich products of the earth, not without the knowledge of letters and many arts, and with large and expensive accommodations for internal intercourse and traffic, has for ages sought to exclude the visits of strangers and foreigners from its dominions, and has assumed for itself a superiority over all other nations. Events appear likely to break down and soften this spirit of nonintercourse and to bring China ere long into the relations which usually subsist between civilized states. She has agreed in the treaty with England that correspondence between the agents of the two Governments shall be on equal terms—a concession which it is hardly probable will hereafter be withheld from other nations.

It is true that the cheapness of labor among the Chinese, their ingenuity in its application, and the fixed character of their habits and pursuits may discourage the hope of the opening of any great and sudden demand for the fabrics of other countries. But experience proves that the productions of western nations find a market to some extent among the Chinese; that the market, so far as respects the productions of the United States, although it has considerably varied in successive seasons, has on the whole more than doubled within the last ten years; and it can hardly be doubted that the opening of several new and important ports connected with parts of the Empire heretofore seldom visited by Europeans or Americans would exercise a favorable influence upon the demand for such productions.

It is not understood that the immediate establishment of correspondent embassies and missions or the permanent residence of diplomatic functionaries with full powers of each country at the Court of the other is contemplated between England and China, although, as has been already observed, it has been stipulated that intercourse between the two countries shall hereafter be on equal terms. An ambassador or envoy extraordinary and minister plenipotentiary can only be accredited, according to the usages of western nations, to the head or sovereign of the state, and it may be doubtful whether the Court of Peking is yet prepared to conform to these usages so far as to receive a minister plenipotentiary to reside near it.

Being of opinion, however, that the commercial interests of the United States connected with China require at the present moment a degree of attention and vigilance such as there is no agent of this Government on the spot to bestow, I recommend to Congress to make appropriation for the compensation of a commissioner to reside in China to exercise a watchful care over the concerns of American citizens and for the protection of their persons and property, empowered to hold intercourse with the local authorities, and ready, under instructions from his Government, should such instructions become necessary and proper hereafter, to address himself to the high functionaries of the Empire, or through them to the Emperor himself.

It will not escape the observation of Congress that in order to secure the important object of any such measure a citizen of much intelligence and weight of character should be employed on such agency, and that to secure the services of such an individual a compensation should be made corresponding with the magnitude and importance of the mission.

JOHN TYLER.

TREATIES AND OTHER INTERNATIONAL AGREEMENTS OF THE UNITED STATES OF AMERICA 1776–1949

(Compiled under the direction of Charles I. Bevans, LL.B., Assistant Legal Adviser, Department of State)

FRIENDSHIP, COMMERCE, AND NAVIGATION

Treaty signed at Washington December 20, 1849
Senate advice and consent to ratification January 14, 1850
Ratified by the President of the United States February 4, 1850
Ratified by the Hawaiian Islands August 19, 1850

Ratifications exchanged at Honolulu August 24, 1850
Entered into force August 24, 1850
Proclaimed by the President of the United States November 9, 1850
Terminated August 12, 1898, upon annexation of Hawaii—9 Stat. 977; Treaty Series 160 [1].

The United States of America and His Majesty the King of the Hawaiian Islands, equally animated with the desire of maintaining the relations of good understanding which have hitherto so happily subsisted between their respective states, and consolidating the commercial intercourse between them, have agreed to enter into negotiations for the conclusion of a Treaty of Friendship, Commerce and Navigation, for which purpose they have appointed plenipotentiaries, that is to say:

The President of the United States of America, John M. Clayton, Secretary of State of the United States; and His Majesty the King of the Hawaiian Islands, James Jackson Jarves, accredited as his Special Commissioner to the Government of the United States; who, after having exchanged their full powers, found in good and due form, have concluded and signed the following articles:

Article I

There shall be perpetual peace and amity between the United States and the King of the Hawaiian Islands, his heirs and his successors.

Article II

There shall be reciprocal liberty of commerce and navigation between the United States of America and the Hawaiian Islands.

No duty of customs, or other impost, shall be charged upon any goods, the produce or manufacture of one country, upon importation from such country into the other, other or higher than the duty or impost charged upon goods of the same kind, the produce or manufacture of, or imported from, any other country; and the United States of America and His Majesty the King of the Hawaiian Islands do hereby engage, that the subjects or citizens of any other state shall not enjoy any favor, privilege, or immunity, whatever, in matters of commerce and navigation, which shall not also, at the same time, be extended to the subjects or citizens of the other contracting party, gratuitously, if the concession in favor of that other State shall have been gratuitous, and in return for a compensation, as nearly as possible of proportionate value and effect, to be adjusted by mutual agreement, if the concession shall have been conditional.

---

[1] For a detailed study of this treaty, see Miller 591.

Article III

All articles the produce or manufacture of either country which can legally be imported into either country from the other, in ships of that other country, and thence coming, shall, when so imported, be subject to the same duties, and enjoy the same privileges, whether imported in ships of the one country, or in ships of the other; and in like manner, all goods which can legally be exported or reexported from either country to the other, in ships of that other country, shall, when so exported or reexported, be subject to the same duties, and be entitled to the same privileges, drawbacks, bounties, and allowances, whether exported in ships of the one country, or in ships of the other: and all goods and articles, of whatever description, not being of the produce or manufacture of the United States, which can be legally imported into the Sandwich Islands, shall when so imported in vessels of the United States pay no other or higher duties, imposts, or charges than shall be payable upon the like goods, and articles, when imported in the vessels of the most favored foreign nation other than the nation of which the said goods and articles are the produce or manufacture.

Article IV

No duties of tonnage, harbor, light-houses, pilotage, quarantine, or other similar duties, of whatever nature, or under whatever denomination, shall be imposed in either country upon the vessels of the other, in respect of voyages between the United States of America and the Hawaiian Islands, if laden, or in respect of any voyage, if in ballast, which shall not be equally imposed in the like cases on national vessels.

Article V

It is hereby declared, that the stipulations of the present treaty are not to be understood as applying to the navigation and carrying trade between one port and another situated in the states of either contracting party, such navigation and trade being reserved exclusively to national vessels.

Article VI

Steam vessels of the United States which may be employed by the Government of the said States, in the carrying of their Public Mails across the Pacific Ocean, or from one port in that ocean to another, shall have free access to the ports of the Sandwich Islands, with the privilege of stopping therein to refit, to refresh, to land passengers and their baggage, and for the transaction of any business pertaining to the public Mail service of the United States, and shall be subject in such ports to no duties of tonnage, harbor, lighthouses, quarantine, or other similar duties of whatever nature of under whatever denomination.

Article VII

The Whaleships of the United States shall have access to the ports of Hilo, Kealakekua and Hanalei in the Sandwich Islands, for the purposes of refitment and refreshment, as well as to the ports of Honolulu and Lahaina which only are ports of entry for all Merchant vessels, and in all the above named ports, they shall be permitted to trade or barter their supplies or goods, excepting spirituous liquors, to be amount of two hundred dollars *ad valorem* for each vessel, without paying any charge for tonnage or harbor dues of any description, or any duties or imposts whatever upon the goods or articles so traded or bartered. They shall also be permitted, with the like exemption from all charges for tonnage and harbor dues, further to trade or barter, with the same exception as to spirituous liquors, to the additional amount of one thousand dollars *ad valorem,* for each vessel, paying upon the additional goods, and articles so traded and bartered, no other or higher duties, than are payable on like goods, and articles, when imported in the vessels and by the citizens or subjects of the most favored foreign nation. They shall also be permitted to pass from port to port of the Sandwich Islands for the purpose of procuring refreshments, but they shall not discharge their seamen or land their passengers in the said Islands, except at Lahaina and Honolulu; and, in all the ports names in this article, the whaleships of the United States shall enjoy in all respects, whatsoever, all the rights, privilege and immunities, which are enjoyed by, or shall be granted to, the whaleships of the most favored foreign nation. The like privilege of frequenting the three ports of the Sandwich Islands, above named in this article, not being ports of entry for merchant vessels, is also guaranteed to all the public armed vessels of the United States. But nothing in this article shall be construed as authorizing any vessel of the United States, having on board any disease usually regarded as requiring quarantine, to enter, during the continuance of such disease on board, any port of the Sandwich Islands, other than Lahaina or Honolulu.

Article VIII

The contracting parties engage, in regard to the personal privileges that the citizens of the United States of America shall enjoy in the dominions of His Majesty the King of the Hawaiian Islands, and the subjects of his said Majesty in the United States of America, that they shall have free and undoubted right to travel and to reside in the states of the two high contracting parties, subject to the same precautions of police which are practiced towards the subjects or citizens of the most favored nations. They shall be entitled to occupy dwellings and warehouses, and to dispose of their personal property of every kind and description, by sale, gift, exchange, will, or in any other way whatever, without the smallest hinderance or obstacle; and their heirs or representatives, being subjects or citizens of the other contracting party, shall succeed to their personal goods, whether by testament or ab intestato; and may take possession thereof, either by themselves or by others acting for them, and dispose of the same at will, paying to the profit of the respective governments such dues only as the inhabitants of the country wherein the said goods are, shall be subject to pay in like cases. And in case of the absence of the heir and representative, such care shall be taken of the said goods as would be taken of the goods of a native of the same country in like case, until the lawful owner may take measures for receiving them. And if a question should arise among several claimants as to which of them said goods belong, the same shall be decided finally by the laws and judges of the land wherein the said goods are. Where on the decease of any person holding real estate within the territories of one party, such real estate would, by the laws of the land, descend on a citizen or subject of the other, were he not disqualified by alienage, such citizen or subject shall be allowed a reasonable time to sell the same, and withdraw the proceeds without molestation, and exempt from all duties of detraction on the part of the government of the respective States. The citizens or subjects of the contracting parties shall not be obliged to pay, under any pretence whatever, any taxes or impositions, other or greater than those which are paid, or may hereafter be paid, by the subjects or citizens of the most favored nations, in the respective states of the high contracting parties. They shall be exempt from all military service, whether by land or by sea; from forced loans, and from every extraordinary contribution not general and by law established. Their dwellings, warehouse, and all premises appertaining thereto, destined for the purposes of commerce or residence, shall be respected. No arbitrary search of, or visit to, heir houses, and no arbitrary examination or inspection whatever of the books, papers, or accounts of their trade, shall be made; but such measures shall be executed only in conformity with the legal sentence of a competent tribunal; and each of the two contracting parties engages that the citizens or subjects of the other residing in their respective states shall enjoy their property and personal security, in as full and ample manner as their own citizens or subjects, or the subjects or citizens of the most favored nation, but subject always to the laws and statutes of the two countries respectively.

Article IX

The citizens and subjects of each of the two contracting parties shall be free in the states of the other to manage their own affairs themselves, or to commit those affairs to the management of any persons whom they may appoint as their broker, factor or agent; nor shall the citizens and subjects of the two contracting parties be restrained in their choice of persons to act in such capacities, nor shall they be called upon to pay any salary or remuneration to any person whom they shall not choose to employ.

Absolute freedom shall be given in all cases to the buyer and seller to bargain together and to fix the price of any goods or merchandise imported into, or to be exported from the states and dominions of the two contracting parties; save and except generally such cases wherein the laws and usages of the country may require the intervention of any special agents in the states and dominions of the contracting parties. But nothing contained in his or any other article of the present Treaty shall be construed to authorize the sale of spirituous liquors to the natives of the Sandwich Islands farther than such sale may be allowed by the Hawaiian laws.

Article X

Each of the two contracting parties may have, in the ports of the other, consuls, vice consuls, and commercial agents, of their own appointment, who shall enjoy the same privileges and powers with those of the most favored nations; but if any such consuls shall exercise commerce, they shall be subject to the same laws and usages to which the private individuals of their nation are subject in the same place. The said Consuls, vice consuls, and commercial agents are authorized to require the assistance of the local authorities for the search, arrest, detention, and imprisonment of the deserters from the ships of war and merchant vessels of their country. For this purpose, they shall apply to the competent tribunals, judges and officers, and shall in writing demand the said deserters, proving, by the exhibition of the registers of the vessels, the rolls of the crews, or by other official documents, that such individuals formed part of the crews; and this reclamation being thus substantiated, the surrender shall not be refused. Such deserters, when arrested shall be placed at the disposal of the said consuls, vice consuls, or commercial agents, and may be confined in the public prisons, at the request and cost of those who shall claim them, in order to be detained until the time when they shall be restored to the vessel to which they belonged, or sent back to their own country by a vessel of the same nation or any other vessel whatsoever. The agents, owners or masters of vessels on account of whom the deserters have been apprehended, upon requisition of the local authorities shall be required to takes or send away such deserters from the states and dominions of the contracting parties, or give such security for their good conduct as the law may require. But if not sent back nor reclaimed within six months from the day of their arrest, or if all the expenses of such imprisonment are not defrayed by the party causing such arrest and imprisonment, they shall be set at liberty and shall not be again arrested by the same cause. However, if the deserters should be found to have committed any crime or offense, their surrender may be delayed until the tribunal before which their case shall be depending, shall have pronounced its sentence, and such sentence shall have been carried into effect.

Article XI

It is agreed that perfect and entire liberty of conscience shall be enjoyed by the citizens and subjects of both the contracting parties, in the countries of the one of the other, without their being liable to be disturbed or molested on account of their religious belief. But nothing contained in this article shall be construed to interfere with the exclusive right of the Hawaiian Government to regulate for itself the Schools which it may establish or support within its jurisdiction.

Article XII

If any ships of war or other vessels, be wrecked on the coasts of the states or territories of either of the contracting parties, such ships or vessels, or any parts thereof, and all furniture and appurtenances belonging thereunto, and all goods and merchandize which shall be saved therefrom, or the produce thereof if sold shall be faithfully restored with the least possible delay to the proprietors, upon being claimed by them, or by their duly authorized factors; and if there are no such proprietors or factors on the spot, then the said goods and merchandize, or the proceeds thereof, as well as all the papers found on board such wrecked ships or vessels, shall be delivered to the American or Hawaiian Consul, or vice consul in whose district the wreck may have taken place; and such Consul, vice consul, proprietors or factors, shall pay only the expenses incurred in the preservation of the property, together with the rate of salvage and expenses of quarantine which would have been payable in the like case of a wreck of a national vessel; and the goods and merchandize saved from the wreck shall not be subject to duties unless entered for consumption; it being understood that in case of any legal claim upon such wreck, goods or merchandize, the same shall be referred for decision to the competent tribunals of the country.

Article XIII

The vessels of either of the two contracting parties which may be forced by stress of weather or other cause into one of the ports of the other, shall be exempt from all duties of port or navigation paid for the benefit of the state, if the motives which led to their seeking refuge be real and evident, and if no cargo be discharged or taken on board, save such as may relate to the subsistence of the crew, or be necessary for the repair of the vessels, and if they do not stay in port beyond the time necessary, keeping in view the cause which led to their seeking refuge.

Article XIV

The contracting parties mutually agree to surrender, upon official requisition, to the authorities of each, all persons who, being charged with the crimes of murder, piracy, arson, robbery, forgery or the utterance of forged paper, committed within the jurisdiction of either, shall be found within the territories of the other; provided, that this shall only be done upon such evidence of criminality as, according to the laws of the place where the person so charged shall be found, would justify his apprehension and commitment for trial if the crime had there been committed: and the respective judges and other magistrates of the two Governments, shall have authority, upon complaint made under oath, to issue a warrant for the apprehension of the person so charged, that he may be brought before such judges or other magistrates respectively, to the end that the evidence of criminality may be heard and considered; and if, on such hearing, the evidence be deemed sufficient to sustain the charge, it shall be the duty of the examining judge or magistrate to certify the same to the proper Executive authority, that a warrant may issue for the surrender of such fugitive. The expense of such apprehension and delivery shall be borne and defrayed by the party who makes the requisition and receives the fugitive.

Article XV

So soon as Steam or other mail Packets under the flag of either of the contracting parties, shall have commenced running between their respective ports of entry, the contracting parties agree to receive at the post offices of those ports all mailable matter, and to forward it as directed, the destination being to some regular post office of either country; charging thereupon the regular postal rates as established by law in the territories of either party receiving said mailable matter, in addition to the original postage of the office whence the mail was sent. Mails for the United States shall be made up at regular intervals at the Hawaiian Post Office, and dispatched to ports of the United States, the postmasters at which ports shall open the same, and forward the enclosed matter as directed, crediting the Hawaiian Government with their postages as established by law and stamped upon each manuscript or printed sheet.

All mailable matter destined for the Hawaiian Islands shall be received at the several post offices in the United States and forwarded to San Francisco or other ports on the Pacific coast of the United States, whence the postmasters shall depatch it by the regular mail packets to Honolulu, the Hawaiian government agreeing on their part to receive and collect for and credit the Post Office Department of the United States with the United States rates charged thereupon. It shall be optional to pre-pay the postage on letters in either country, but postage on printed sheets and newspapers shall in all case be pre-paid. The respective post office Departments of the contracting parties shall in their accounts, which are to be adjusted annually, be credited with all dead letters returned.

Article XVI

The present treaty shall be in force from the date of the exchange of the ratifications for the term of ten years, and further, until the end of twelve months after either of the contracting parties shall have given notice to the other of its intention to terminate the same, each of the said contracting parties reserving to itself the right of giving such notice at the end of the said term of ten years, or at any subsequent term.

Any citizen or subject of either party infringing the articles of this treaty shall be held responsible for the same and the harmony and good correspondence between the two governments shall not be interrupted thereby, each party engaging in no way to protect the offender or sanction such violation.

Article XVII

The present treaty shall be ratified by the President of the United States of America, by and with the advice and consent of the Senate of the said States, and by His Majesty the King of the Hawaiian Islands, by and with the advice of this Privy Council of State, and the ratifications shall be exchanged at Honolulu within eighteen months from the date of its signature, or sooner if possible.

In witness whereof, the respective Plenipotentiaries have signed the same in triplicate, and have thereto affix their seals. Done at Washington in the English language, the twentieth day of December, in the year one thousand eight hundred and forty nine.

JOHN M. CLAYTON.
JAMES JACKSON JARVES.

TREATIES AND OTHER INTERNATIONAL AGREEMENTS OF THE UNITED STATES OF AMERICA 1776–1949

(Compiled under the direction of Charles I. Bevans, LL.B. Assistant Legal Adviser, Department of State)

COMMERCIAL RECIPROCITY

Convention signed at Washington January 30, 1875
Senate advice and consent to ratification, with amendments, March 18, 1875 [1]

---

[1] The Senate resolution contained the following amendments:
Art. I. After the words "being the growth" insert the word "and"; in the schedule delete the word "fruits" and insert the word "Bananas"; after the word "Pulu" delete the words "Sandal, Koa, or other ornamental woods".
Art. II. At the end of the schedule add "; harness and all manufactures of leather; starch; and tobacco, whether in leaf or manufactured".

Continued

Ratified by the Hawaiian Islands April 17, 1875
Ratified by the President of the United States, with amendments, May 31, 1875 [1]
Ratifications exchanged at Washington, June 3, 1875
Proclaimed by the President of the United States June 3, 1875
Entered into force September 9, 1876
Supplemented by convention of December 6, 1884 [2]
Terminated August 12, 1898, upon annexation of Hawaii—19 Stat. 625; Treaty Series 161.

CONVENTION

The United States of American and His Majesty the King of the Hawaiian Islands, equally animated by the desire to strengthen and perpetuate the friendly relations which have heretofore uniformly existed between them, and to consolidate their commercial intercourse, have resolved to enter into a Convention for Commercial Reciprocity. For this purpose, the President of the United States has conferred full powers on Hamilton Fish, Secretary of State, and His Majesty the King of the Hawaiian Islands has conferred like powers on Honorable Elisha H. Allen, Chief Justice of the Supreme Court, Chancellor of the Kingdom, Member of the Privy Council of State, His Majesty's Envoy Extraordinary and Minister Plenipotentiary to the United States of America, and Honorable Henry A. P. Carter, Member of the Privy Council of State, His Majesty's Special Commissioner to the United States of America.

And the said Plenipotentiaries, after having exchanged their full powers, which were found to be in due form, have agreed to the following articles:

Article I

For and in consideration of the rights and privileges granted by His Majesty the King of the Hawaiian Islands in the next succeeding article of this convention, and as an equivalent therefor, the United States of America hereby agree to admit all the articles named in the following schedule, the same being the growth and manufacture or produce of the Hawaiian Islands, into all the ports of the United States free of duty.

Schedule

Arrow-root; castor oil; bananas, nuts, vegetables, dried and undried, preserved and unpreserved; hides and skins

---

Art. IV. At the end of the article add the following sentence: "It is agreed, on the part of His Hawaiian Majesty, that, so long as this treaty shall remain in force, he will not lease or otherwise dispose of or create any lien upon any port, harbor, or other territory in his dominions, or grant any special privilege or rights of use therein, to any other power, state or government, nor make any treaty by which any other nation shall obtain the same privileges, relative to the admission of any articles free of duty, hereby secured to the United States".

Art. V. After "Government of the United States" delete the words "and the laws required" and insert in lieu thereof "but not until a law".

The text printed here is the amended text as proclaimed by the President.

[2] TS 163, *post*, p. 878.

undressed; rice; pulu; seeds, plants, shrubs or trees; muscovado, brown, and all other unrefined sugar meaning hereby the grades of sugar heretofore commonly imported from the Hawaiian Islands and now known in the markets of San Francisco and Portland as "Sandwich Island sugar;" syrups of sugar-cane, melado, and molasses; tallow.

Article II

For and in consideration of the rights and privileges granted by the United States of America in the preceding article of this convention, and as an equivalent therefor, His Majesty the King of the Hawaiian Islands hereby agrees to admit all the articles named in the following schedule, the same being the growth, manufacture, or produce of the United States of America, into all the ports of the Hawaiian Islands free of duty.

Schedule

Agricultural implements; animals, beef, bacon, pork, ham and all fresh, smoked or preserved meats; boots and shoes; grain, flour, meal and bran, bread and breadstuffs, of all kinds; bricks, lime and cement; butter, cheese, lard, tallow, bullion, coal; cordage, naval stores including tar, pitch, resin, turpentine raw and rectified; copper and composition sheathing; nails and bolts; cotton and manufactures of cotton bleached, and unbleached, and whether or not colored, stained, painted or printed; eggs; fish and oysters, and all other creatures living in the water, and the products thereof; fruits, nuts and vegetables, green, dried or undried, preserved or unpreserved; hardware; hides, furs, skins and pelts, dressed or undressed; hoop iron, and rivets, nails, spikes and bolts, tacks, brads or sprigs; ice; iron and steel and manufactures thereof; leather; lumber and timber of all kinds, round, hewed, sawed, and unmanufactured in whole or in part; doors, sashes and blinds; machinery of all kinds, engines and parts thereof; oats and hay; paper, stationery and books, and all manufactures of paper or of paper and wood; petroleum and all oils for lubricating or illuminating purposes; plants, shrubs, trees and seeds; rice; sugar, refined or unrefined; salt; soap; shooks, staves and headings; wool and manufactures of wool, other than ready made clothing; wagons and carts for the purposes of agriculture or of drayage; wood and manufactures of wood, or of wood and metal except furniture either upholstered or carved and carriages; textile manufactures, made of a combination of wool, cotton, silk or linen, or of any two or more of them other than when ready made clothing; harness and all manufactures of leather; starch; and tobacco, whether in leaf or manufactured.

Article III

The evidence that articles proposed to be admitted into the ports of the United States of America, or the ports of the Hawaiian Islands, free of duty, under the first and second articles of this convention, are the growth, manufacture or produce of the United States of America or of the Hawaiian Islands respectively shall be established under such rules and regulations and conditions for the protection of the revenue as the two Governments may from time to time respectively prescribe.

Article IV

No export duty or charges shall be imposed in the Hawaiian Islands or in the United States, upon any of the articles proposed to be admitted into the ports of the United States or the ports of the Hawaiian Islands free of duty, under the First and Second Articles of this convention. It is agreed, on the part of His Hawaiian Majesty, that, so long as this treaty shall remain in force, he will not lease or otherwise dispose of or create any lien upon any port, harbor, or other territory in his dominions, or grant any special privilege or rights of use therein, to any other power, state or government, nor make any treaty by which any other nation shall obtain the same privileges, relative to the admission of any articles free of duty, hereby secured to the United States.

Article V

The present convention shall take effect as soon as it shall have been approved and proclaimed by His Majesty the King of the Hawaiian Islands, and shall have been ratified and duly proclaimed on the part of the Government of the United States, but not until a law to carry it into operation shall have been passed by the Congress of the United States of America. Such assent having been given and the ratifications of the convention having been exchanged as provided in article VI, the convention shall remain in force for seven years, from the date at which it may come into operation; and further, until the expiration of twelve months after either of the high contracting parties shall give notice to the other of its wish to terminate the same; each of the high contracting parties being at liberty to give such notice to the other at the end of the said term of seven years, or at any time thereafter.

Article VI

The present convention shall be duly ratified, and the ratifications exchanged at Washington city, within eighteen months from the date hereof, or earlier if possible.

In faith whereof the respective Plenipotentiaries of the high contracting parties have signed this present convention, and have affixed thereto their respective seals.

Done in duplicate, at Washington, the thirtieth day of January, in the year of our Lord, one thousand eight hundred and seventy-five.

HAMILTON FISH.
ELISHA H. ALLEN.
HENRY A. P. CARTER.

THE STATUTES AT LARGE OF THE UNITED STATES OF AMERICA, FROM DECEMBER, 1887, TO MARCH, 1889, AND RECENT TREATIES, POSTAL CONVENTIONS, AND EXECUTIVE PROCLAMATIONS

Supplementary Convention between the United States of America and his Majesty the King of the Hawaiian Islands to limit the duration of the Convention respecting commercial reciprocity concluded January 30, 1875. Concluded December 6, 1884; ratification advised by the Senate with amendments, January 20, 1887; ratified by the President November 7, 1887; ratified by the King of Hawaii, October 20, 1887; ratifications exchanged at Washington November 9, 1887; proclaimed November 8, 1887.

BY THE PRESIDENT OF THE UNITED STATES OF AMERICA

A PROCLAMATION

Whereas a Convention between the United States of America and the Kingdom of the Hawaiian Islands, for the purpose of definitely limiting the duration of the Convention concerning Commercial Reciprocity concluded between the same High Contracting Parties on the thirtieth day of January 1875, was concluded and signed by their respective plenipotentiaries at the city of Washington, on the sixth day of December, in the year of our Lord, 1884, which Convention, as amended by the Senate of the United States and being in the English language, is word for word as follows:

Supplementary Convention to limit the duration of the Convention respecting commercial reciprocity between the United States of America and the Hawaiian Kingdom, concluded January 30, 1875.

Whereas a Convention was concluded between the United States of America, and His Majesty the King of the Hawaiian Islands, on the thirtieth day of January 1875, concerning commercial reciprocity, which by the fifth article thereof, was to continue in force for seven years from the date after it was to come into operation and further, until the expiration of twelve months after either of the High Contracting Parties should give notice to the other of its wish to terminate the same; and

Whereas, the High Contracting Parties consider that the increase and consolidation of their mutual commercial interests would be better promoted by the definite limitation of the duration of the said Convention;

Therefore, the President of the United States of America, and His Majesty the King of the Hawaiian Islands, have appointed: The President of the United States of America, Frederick T. Frelinghuysen, Secretary of State; and His Majesty the King of the Hawaiian Islands, Henry A.P. Carter, accredited to the Government of the United

States as His Majesty's Envoy Extraordinary and Minister Plenipotentiaries; who, having exchanged their respective powers, which were found sufficiently and in due form, have agreed upon the following articles:

Article I

The High Contracting Parties agree, that the time fixed for the duration of the said Convention, shall be definitely extended for a term of seven years from the date of the exchange of ratifications hereof, and further, until the expiration of twelve months after either of the High Contracting Parties shall give notice to the other of its wish to terminate the same, each of the High Contracting Parties being at liberty to give such notice to the other at the end of the said term of seven years or at any time thereafter.

Article II

His Majesty the King of the Hawaiian Islands grants to the Government of the United States the exclusive right to enter the harbor of Peal River, in the Island of Oahu, and to establish and maintain there a coaling and repair station for the use of vessels of the United States, and to that end the United States may improve the entrance to said harbor and do all other things needful to the purpose aforesaid.

Article III

The present Convention shall be ratified and the ratifications exchanged at Washington, as soon as possible.

In witness whereof, the respective Plenipotentiaries have signed the present Convention in duplicate, and have hereunto affixed their respective seals.

Done at the city of Washington the 6th day of December in the year of our Lord 1884.

      FREDK. T. FRELINGHUYSEN.
      HENRY A. P. CARTER.

And whereas the said Convention, as amended, has been duty ratified on both parts, and the respective ratifications of the same have been exchanged.

Now, therefore, be it known that I, Grover Cleveland, President of the United States of America, have caused the said Convention to be made public to the end that the same and every article and clause thereof, as amended, may be observed and fulfilled with good faith by the United States and the citizens thereof.

In testimony whereof, I have hereunto set my hand and caused the seal of the United States to be affixed.

Done at the city of Washington this ninth day of November in the year of our Lord one thousand eight hundred and eighty-seven and the Independence of the United States the one hundred and twelfth.

      GROVER CLEVELAND.

By the President: T.F. BAYARD, *Secretary of State.*

By 1893, Queen Liliuokalani was the ruling monarch of the Hawaiian Islands. The eighth Native Hawaiian ruler of the Kingdom of Hawaii, she would eventually become its last.

As American business interests, particularly in the sugar and pineapple industries, flourished in the Hawaiian Islands with the expansion of trade and political ties with the United States, so did their political interests and ambitions in the Hawaiian Islands. On January 17, 1893, Queen Liliuokalani was overthrown by a "Committee of Safety" that represented American and European sugar planters, descendants of missionaries, and financiers. The "Committee of Safety," which proclaimed the establishment of a Provisional Government on the same day, was immediately extended diplomatic recognition by the U.S. Minister to the Kingdom of Hawaii without the consent of Queen Liliuokalani or the Native Hawaiian people.

Without the active support and military intervention by U.S. diplomatic and military representatives, who caused over 100 marines to invade the Kingdom of Hawaii and position themselves near government buildings and the Queen's palace on January 16, 1893, to intimidate the Queen and her government, the insurrection would have failed for lack of popular support and insufficient arms.

The Provisional Government, which later declared itself to be the Republic of Hawaii on July 4, 1894, sought immediate annexation by the United States after the overthrow. In a message to Congress on December 18, 1893, President Grover Cleveland detailed the illegal actions of the Provisional Government which led to the overthrow of the Kingdom of Hawaii, and explained why he opposed the submission of a treaty of annexation to the Senate. President Cleveland's message is as follows:

PRESIDENT'S MESSAGE RELATING TO THE
HAWAIIAN ISLANDS—DECEMBER 18, 1893

MESSAGE

To the Senate and House of Representatives:

In my recent annual message to the Congress I briefly referred to our relations with Hawaii and expressed the intention of transmitting further information on the subject when additional advices permitted.

Though I am not able now to report a definite change in the actual situation, I am convinced that the difficulties lately created both here and in Hawaii and now standing in the way of a solution through Executive action of the problem presented, render it proper, and expedient, that the matter should be referred to the broader authority and discretion of Congress, with a full explanation of the endeavor thus far made to deal with the emergency and a statement of the considerations which have governed my action.

I suppose that right and justice should determine the path to be followed in treating this subject. If national honesty is to be disregarded and a desire for territorial extension, or dissatisfaction with a form of government not our own, ought to regulate our conduct, I have entirely misapprehended the mission and character of our Government and the behavior which the conscience of our people demands of their public servants.

When the present Administration entered upon its duties the Senate had under consideration a treaty providing for the annexation of the Hawaiian Islands to the territory of the United States. Surely under our Constitution and laws the enlargement of our limits is a manifestation of the highest attribute of sovereignty, and if entered upon as an Executive act, all things relating to the transaction should be clear and free from suspicion. Additional importance attached to this particular treaty of annexation, because it contemplated a departure from unbroken American tradition in providing for the addition to our territory of islands of the sea more than two thousand miles removed from our nearest coast.

These considerations might not of themselves call for interference with the completion of a treaty entered upon by a previous Administration. But it appeared from the documents accompanying the treaty when submitted to the Senate, that the ownership of Hawaii was tendered to us by a provisional government set up to succeed the constitutional ruler of the islands, who had been dethroned, and it did not appear that such provisional government had the sanction of either popular revolution or suffrage. Two other remarkable features of the transaction naturally attracted attention. One was the extraordinary haste—not to say precipitancy—characterizing all the transactions connected with the treaty. It appeared that a so-called Committee of Safety, ostensibly the source of the revolt against the constitutional Government of Hawaii, was organized on Saturday, the 14th day of January; that on Monday, the 16th, the United States forces were landed at Honolulu from a naval vessel lying in its harbor; that on the 17th the scheme of a provisional government was perfected, and a proclamation naming its officers was on the same day prepared and read at the Government building; that immediately thereupon the United States Minister recognized the provisional government thus created; that two days afterwards, on the 19th day of January, commissioners representing such government sailed for this country in a steamer especially chartered for the occasion, arriving in San Francisco on the 28th day of January, and in Washington on the 3d day of February; that on the next day they had their first interview with the Secretary of State, and another on the 11th, when the treaty of annexation was practically agreed upon, and that on the 14th it was formally concluded and on the 15th transmitted to the Senate. Thus between the initiation of the scheme for a provisional government in Hawaii on the 14th day of January and the submission to the Senate of the treaty of annexation concluded with such government, the entire interval was thirty-two days, fifteen of which were spent by the Hawaiian Commissioners in their journey to Washington.

In the next place, upon the face of the papers submitted with the treaty, it clearly appeared that there was open and undetermined an issue of fact of the most vital importance. The message of the President accompanying the treaty declared that "the overthrow of the monarchy was not in any way promoted by this Government," and in a letter to the President from the Secretary of State, also submitted to the Senate with the treaty, the following passage occurs: "At the time the provisional government took possession of the Government buildings no troops or officers of the United States were present or took any part whatever in the proceedings. No public recognition was accorded to the provisional government by the United States Minister until after the Queen's abdication and when they were in effective possession of the Government buildings, the archives, the treasury, the barracks, the police station, and all the potential machinery of the Government." But a protest also accompanied said treaty, signed by the Queen and her ministers at the time she made way for the provisional government, which explicitly stated that she yielded to the superior force of the United States, whose Minister had caused United States troops to be landed at Honolulu and declared that he would support such provisional government.

The truth or falsity of this protest was surely of the first importance. If true, nothing but the concealment of its truth could induce our Government to negotiate with the semblance of a government thus created, nor could a treaty resulting from the acts stated in the protest have been knowingly deemed worthy of consideration by the Senate. Yet the truth or falsity of the protest had not been investigated.

I conceived it to be my duty therefore to withdraw the treaty from the Senate for examination, and meanwhile to cause an accurate, full, and impartial investigation to be made of the facts attending the subversion of the constitutional Government of Hawaii, and the installment in its place of the provisional government. I selected for the work of investigation the Hon. James H. Blount, of Georgia, whose service of eighteen years as a member of the House of Representatives, and whose experience as chairman of the Committee of Foreign Affairs in that body, and his consequent familiarity with international topics, joined with his high character and honorable reputation, seemed to render him peculiarly fitted for the duties entrusted to him. His report detailing his action under the instructions given to him and the conclusions derived from his investigation accompany this message.

These conclusions do not rest for their acceptance entirely upon Mr. Blount's honesty and ability as a man; nor upon his acumen and impartiality as an investigator. They are accompanied by the evidence upon which they are based, which evidence is also here-with transmitted, and from which it seems to me no other deductions could possibly be reached than those arrived at by the Commissioner.

The report with its accompanying proofs, and such other evidence as is now before the Congress or is herewith submitted, justifies in my opinion the statement that when the President was led to submit the treaty to the Senate with the declaration that "the overthrow of the monarchy was not in any way promoted by this Government", and when the Senate was induced to receive and discuss it on that basis, both President and Senate were misled.

The attempt will not be made in this communication to touch upon all facts which throw light upon the progress and consummation of this scheme of annexation. A very brief and imperfect reference to the facts and evidence at hand will exhibit its character and the incidents in which it had its birth.

It is unnecessary to set forth the reasons which in January, 1893, led a considerable proportion of American and other foreign merchants and traders residing at Honolulu to favor the annexation of Hawaii to the United States. It is sufficient to note the fact and to observe that the project was one which was zealously promoted by the Minister representing the United States in that country. He evidently had an ardent desire that it should become a fact accomplished by his agency and during his ministry, and was not inconveniently scrupulous as to the means employed to that end. On the 19th day of November, 1892, nearly two months before the first overt act tending towards the subversion of the Hawaiian Government and the attempted transfer of Hawaiian Government and the attempted transfer of Hawaiian territory to the United States, he addressed a long letter to the Secretary of State in which the case for annexation was elaborately argued, on moral, political, and economical grounds. He refers to the loss to the Hawaiian sugar interest from the operation of the McKinley bill, and the tendency to still further depreciation of sugar property unless some positive measure of relief is granted. He strongly inveighs against the existing Hawaiian Government and emphatically declares for annexation. He says: "In truth the monarchy here is an absurd anachronism. It has nothing on which it logically or legitimately stands. The feudal basis on which it once stood no longer existing, the monarchy now is only an impediment to good government—an obstruction to the prosperity and progress of the islands."

He further says: "As a crown colony of Great Britain or a Territory of the United States the government modifications could be made readily and good administration of the law secured. Destiny and the vast future interests of the United States in the Pacific clearly indicate who at no distant day must be responsible for the government of these islands. Under a territorial government they could be as easily governed as any of the existing Territories of the United States." * * * "Hawaii has reached the parting of the ways. She must not take the road which leads to Asia, or the other which outlets her in America, gives her an American civilization, and binds her to the care of American destiny." He also declares: "One of two courses seems to me absolutely necessary to be followed, either bold and vigorous measures for annexation or a 'customs union,' an ocean cable from the California coast to Honolulu, Pearl Harbor perpetually ceded to the United States, with an implied but not expressly stipulated American protectorate over the islands. I believe the former to be the better, that which will prove much the more advantageous to the islands, and the cheapest and least embarrassing in the end to the United States. If it was wise for the United States through Secretary Marcy thirty-eight years ago to offer to expend $100,000 to secure a treaty of annexation, it certainly can not be chimerical or unwise to expend $100,000 to secure annexation in the near future. To-day the United States has five times the wealth she possessed in 1854, and the reasons now existing for annexation are much stronger than they were then. I can not refrain from expressing the opinion with emphasis that the golden hour is near at hand."

These declarations certainly show a disposition and condition of mind, which may be usefully recalled when interpreting the significance of the Minister's conceded acts or when interpreting the significance of the Minister's conceded acts or when considering the probabilities of such conduct on his part as may not be admitted.

In this view it seems proper to also quote from a letter written by the Minister to the Secretary of State on the 8th day of March, 1892, nearly a year prior to the first step taken toward annexation. After stating the possibility that the existing Government of Hawaii might be overturned by an orderly and peaceful revolution, Minister Stevens writes as follows: "Ordinarily in like circumstances, the rule seems to be to limit the landing and movement of United States forces in foreign waters and dominion exclusively to the protection of the United States legation and of the lives and property of American citizens. But as the relations of the United States to Hawaii are exceptional, and in former years the United States officials here took somewhat exceptional action in circumstances of disorder, I desire to know how far the present Minister and naval commander may deviate from established international rules and precedents in the contingencies indicated in the first part of this dispatch."

To a minister of this temper full of zeal for annexation there seemed to arise in January, 1893, the precise opportunity for which he was watchfully waiting—an opportunity which by timely "deviation from established international rules and precedents" might be improved to successfully accomplish the great object in view; and we are quite prepared for the exultant enthusiasm with which in a letter to the State Department date February 1, 1893, he declares: "The Hawaiian pear is now fully ripe and this is the golden hour for the United States to pluck it."

As a further illustration of the activity of this diplomatic representative, attention is called to the fact that on the day the above letter was written, apparently unable longer to restrain his ardor, he issued a proclamation whereby "in the name of the United States" he assumed the protection of the Hawaiian Islands and declared that said action was "taken pending and subject to negotiations at Washington." Of course this assumption of a protectorate was promptly disavowed by our Government, but the American flag remained over the Government building at Honolulu and the forces remained on guard until April, and after Mr. Blount's arrival on the scene, when both were removed.

A brief statement of the occurrences that led to the subversion of the Constitutional Government of Hawaii in the interests of annexation to the United States will exhibit the true complexion of that transaction.

On Saturday, January 14, 1893, the Queen of Hawaii who had been contemplating the proclamation of a new constitution, had, in deference to the wishes and remonstrances of her cabinet, renounced the project for the present at least. Taking this relinquished purpose as a basis of action, citizens of Honolulu numbering from fifty to one hundred, mostly resident aliens, met in a private office and selected a so-called Committee of Safety, composed of thirteen persons, seven of whom were foreign subjects, and consisted of five Americans, one Englishman, and one German. This committee, though its designs were not revealed, had in view nothing less than annexation to the United States, and between Saturday, the 14th, and the following Monday, the 16th of January—though exactly what action was taken may not be clearly disclosed—they were certainly in communication with the United States Minister. On Monday morning the Queen and her cabinet made public proclamation, with a notice which was specially served upon the representatives of all foreign governments, that any changes in the constitution would be sought only in the methods provided by that instrument. Nevertheless, at the call and under the auspices of the Committee of Safety, a mass meeting of citizens was held on that day to protest against the Queen's alleged illegal and unlawful proceedings and purposes. Even at this meeting the Committee of Safety continued to disguise their real purpose and contended themselves with procuring the passage of a resolution denouncing the Queen and empowering the committee to devise ways and means "to secure the permanent maintenance of law and order and the protection of life, liberty, and property in Hawaii." This meeting adjourned between three and four o'clock in the afternoon. On the same day, and immediately after such adjournment, the committee, unwilling to take further steps without the cooperation of the United States Minister, addressed him a note representing that the public safety was menaced and that lives and property were in danger, and concluded as follows:

"We are unable to protect ourselves without aid, and therefore pray for the protection of the United States forces." Whatever may be thought of the other contents of this note, the absolute truth of this latter statement is incontestable. When the note was written and delivered, the committee, so far as it appears, had neither a man nor a gun at their command, and after its delivery they became so panic-stricken at their position that they sent some of their number to interview the Minister and request him not to land the United States forces till the next morning. But he replied that the troops had been ordered, and whether the committee were ready or not the landing should take place. And so it happened that on the 16th day of January, 1893, between four and five o'clock in the afternoon, a detachment of marines from the United States steamer *Boston,* with two pieces of artillery, landed at Honolulu. The men, upwards of 160 in all, were supplied with double cartridge belts filled with ammunition and with haversacks and canteens, and were accompanied by a hospital corps with stretchers and medical supplies. This military demonstration upon the soil of Honolulu was of itself an act of war, unless made either with the consent of the Government of Hawaii or for the *bona fide* purpose of protecting the imperilled lives and property of citizens of the United States. But there is no pretense of any such consent on the part of the Government of the Queen, which at that time was undisputed and was both the *de facto* and the *de jure* government. In point of fact the existing government instead of requesting the presence of an armed force protested against it. There is as little basis for the pretense that such forces were landed for the security of American life and property. If so, they would have been stationed in the vicinity of such property and so as to protect it, instead of at a distance and so as to command the Hawaiian Government building and palace. Admiral Skerrett, the officer in command of our naval force on the Pacific station, has frankly stated that in his opinion the location of the troops was inadvisable if they were landed for the protection of American citizens whose residences and places of business, as well as the legation and consulate, were in a distant part of the city, but the location selected was a wise one if the forces were landed for the purpose of supporting the provisional government. If any peril to life and property calling for any such martial array had existed, Great Britain and other foreign powers interested would not have been behind the United States in activity to protect their citizens. But they made no sign in that direction. When these armed men were landed, the city of Honolulu was in its customary orderly and peaceful condition. There was no symptom of riot or disturbance in any quarter. Men, women, and children were about the streets as usual, and nothing varied the ordinary routine or disturbed the ordinary tranquillity, except the landing of the *Boston's* marines and their march through the town to the quarters assigned them. Indeed, the fact that after having called for the landing of the United States forces on the plea of danger to life and property the Committee of Safety themselves requested the Minister to postpone action, exposed the untruthfulness of their representations of present peril to life and property. The peril they saw was an anticipation growing out of guilty intentions on their part and something which, though not then existing, they knew would certainly follow their attempt to overthrow the Government of the Queen without the aid of the United States forces.

Thus it appears that Hawaii was taken possession of by the United States forces without the consent or wish of the government of the islands, or of anybody else so far as shown, except the United States Minister.

Therefore the military occupation of Honolulu by the United States on the day mentioned was wholly without justification, either as an occupation by consent or as an occupation necessitated by dangers threatening American life and property. It must be accounted for in some other way and on some other ground, and its real motive and purpose are neither obscure nor far to seek.

The United States forces being now on the scene and favorably stationed, the committee proceeded to carry out their original scheme. They met the next morning, Tuesday, the 17th, perfected the plan of temporary government, and fixed upon its principal officers, ten of whom were drawn from the thirteen members of the Committee of Safety. Between one and two o'clock, by squads and by different routes to avoid notice, and having first taken the precaution of ascertaining whether there was any one there to oppose them, they proceeded to the Government building to proclaim the new government. No sign of opposition was manifest, and thereupon an American citizen began to read the proclamation from the steps of the Government building almost entirely without auditors. It is said that before the reading was finished quite a concourse of persons, variously estimated at from 50 to 100, some armed and some unarmed, gathered about the committee to give them aid and confidence. This statement is not important, since the one controlling factor in the whole affair was unquestionably the United States marines, who, drawn up under arms and with artillery in readiness only seventy-six yards distant, dominated the situation.

The provisional government thus proclaimed was by the terms of the proclamation "to exist until terms of union with the United States had been negotiated and agreed upon". The United States Minister, pursuant to prior agreement, recognized this government within an hour after the reading of the proclamation, and before five o'clock, in answer to an inquiry on behalf of the Queen and her cabinet, announced that he had done so.

When our Minister recognized the provisional government the only basis upon which it rested was the fact that the Committee of Safety had in the manner above stated declared it to exist. It was neither a government *de facto* nor *de jure*. That it was not in such possession of the Government property and agencies as entitled it to recognition is conclusively proved by a note found in the files of the Legation at Honolulu, addressed by the declared head of the provisional government to Minister Stevens, dated January 17, 1893, in which he acknowledges with expressions of appreciation the Minister's recognition of the provisional government, and states that it is not yet in the possession of the station house (the place where a large number of the Queen's troops were quartered), though the same had been demanded of the Queen's officers in charge. Nevertheless, this wrongful recognition by our Minister placed the government of the Queen in a position of most perilous perplexity. On the one hand she had possession of the palace, of the barracks, and of the police station, and had at her command at least five hundred fully armed men and several pieces of artillery. Indeed, the whole military force of her kingdom was on her side and at her disposal, while the Committee of Safety, by actual search, had discovered that there were but very few arms in Honolulu that were not in the service of the Government. In this state of things if the Queen could have dealt with the insurgents alone her course would have been plain and the result unmistakable. But the United States had allied itself with her enemies, had recognized them as the true Government of Hawaii, and had put her and her adherents in the position of opposition against lawful authority. She knew that she could not withstand the power of the United States, but she believed that she might safely trust to its justice. Accordingly, some hours after the recognition of the provisional government by the United States Minister, the palace, the barracks, and the police station, with all the military resources of the country, were delivered up by the Queen upon the representation made to her that her cause would thereafter be reviewed at Washington, and while protesting that she surrendered to the superior force of the United States, whose Minister had caused United States troops to be landed at Honolulu and declared that he would support the provisional government, and that she yielded her authority to prevent collision of armed forces and loss of life and only until such time as the United States, upon the facts being presented to it, should undo the action of its representative and reinstate her in the authority she claimed as the constitutional sovereign of the Hawaiian Islands.

This protest was delivered to the chief of the provisional government, who endorsed thereon his acknowledgement of its receipt. The terms of the protest were read without dissent by those assuming to constitute the provisional government, who were certainly charged with the knowledge that the Queen instead of finally abandoning her power had appealed to the justice of the United States for reinstatement in her authority; and yet the provisional government with this unanswered protest in its hand hastened to negotiate with the United States for the permanent banishment of the Queen from power and for a sale of her kingdom.

Our country was in danger of occupying the position of having actually set up a temporary government on foreign soil for the purpose of acquiring through that agency territory which we had wrongfully put in its possession. The control of both sides of a bargain acquired in such a manner is called by a familiar and unpleasant name when found in private transactions. We are not without a precedent showing how scrupulously we avoided such accusations in former days. After the people of Texas had declared their independence of Mexico they resolved that on the acknowledgment of their independence by the United States they would seek admission into the Union. Several months after the battle of San Jacinto, by which Texan independence was practically assured and established, President Jackson declined to recognize it, alleging as one of his reasons that in the circumstances it became us "to beware of a too early movement, as it might subject us, however unjustly, to the imputation of seeking to establish the claim of our neighbors to a territory with a view to its subsequent acquisition by ourselves". This is in marked contrast with the hasty recognition of a government openly and concededly set up for the purpose of tendering to us territorial annexation.

I believe that a candid and thorough examination of the facts will force the conviction that the provisional government owes its existence to an armed invasion by the United States. Fair-minded people with the evidence before them will hardly claim that the Hawaiian Government was overthrown by the people of the islands or that the provisional government had ever existed with their consent. I do not understand that any member of this government claims that the people would uphold it by their suffrages if they were allowed to vote on the question.

While naturally sympathizing with every effort to establish a republican form of government, it has been the settled policy of the United States to concede to people of foreign countries the same freedom and independence in the management of their domestic affairs that we have always claimed for ourselves; and it has been our practice to recognize revolutionary governments as soon as it became apparent that they were supported by the people. For illustration of this rule I need only to refer to the revolution in Brazil in 1889, when our Minister was instructed to recognize the Republic "so soon as a majority of the people of

Brazil should have signified their assent to its establishment and maintenance"; to the revolution in Chile in 1891, when our Minister was directed to recognize the new government "if it was accepted by the people"; and to the revolution in Venezuela in 1892, when our recognition was accorded on condition that the new government was "fully established, in possession of the power of the nation, and accepted by the people."

As I apprehend the situation, we are brought face to face with the following conditions:

The lawful Government of Hawaii was overthrown without the drawing of a sword or the firing of a shot by a process every step of which, it may safely be asserted, is directly traceable to and dependent for its success upon the agency of the United States acting through its diplomatic and naval representatives.

But for the notorious predilections of the United States Minister for annexation, the Committee of Safety, which should be called the Committee of Annexation, would never have existed.

But for the landing of the United States forces upon false pretexts respecting the danger to life and property the committee would never have exposed themselves to the pains and penalties of treason by undertaking the subversion of the Queen's government.

But for the presence of the United States forces in the immediate vicinity and in position to afford all needed protection and support the committee would not have proclaimed the provisional government from the steps of the Government building.

And finally, but for the lawless occupation of Honolulu under false pretexts by the United States forces, and but for Minister Stevens's recognition of the provisional government when the United States forces were its sole support and constituted its only military strength, the Queen and her Government would never have yielded to the provisional government, even for a time and for the sole purpose of submitting her case to the enlightened justice of the United States.

Believing, therefore, that the United States could not, under the circumstances disclosed, annex the islands without justly incurring the imputation of acquiring them by unjustifiable methods, I shall not again submit the treaty of annexation to the Senate for its consideration, and in the instructions to Minister Willis, a copy of which accompanies this message, I have directed him to so inform the provisional government.

But in the present instance our duty does not, in my opinion, end with refusing to consummate this questionable transaction. It has been the boast of our Government that it seeks to do justice in all things without regard to the strength or weakness of those with whom it deals. I mistake the American people if they favor the odious doctrine that there is no such thing as international morality, that there is one law for a strong nation and another for a weak one, and that even by indirection a strong power may with impunity despoil a weak one of its territory.

By an act of war, committed with the participation of a diplomatic representative of the United States and without authority of Congress, the Government of a feeble but friendly and confiding people has been overthrown. A substantial wrong has thus been done which a due regard for our national character as well as the rights of the injured people requires we should endeavor to repair. The provisional government has not assumed a republican or other constitutional form, but has remained a mere executive council or oligarchy, set up without the assent of the people. It has not sought to find a permanent basis of popular support and has given no evidence of an intention to do so. Indeed, the representatives of that government assert that the people of Hawaii are unfit for popular government and frankly avow that they can be best ruled by arbitrary or despotic power.

The law of nations is founded upon reason and justice, and the rules of conduct governing individual relations between citizens or subjects of a civilized state are equally applicable as between enlightened nations. The considerations that international law is without a court for its enforcement, and that obedience to its commands practically depends upon good faith, instead of upon the mandate of a superior tribunal, only give additional sanction to the law itself and brand any deliberate infraction of it not merely as a wrong but as a disgrace. A man of true honor protects the unwritten word which binds his conscience more scrupulously, if possible, than he does the bond a breach of which subjects him to legal liabilities; and the United States in aiming to maintain itself as one of the most enlightened of nations would do its citizens gross injustice if it applied to its international relations any other than a high standard of honor and morality. On that ground the United States can not properly be put in the position of countenancing a wrong after its commission any more than in that of consenting to it in advance. On that ground it can not allow itself to refuse to redress an injury inflicted through an abuse of power by officers clothed with its authority and wearing its uniform; and on the same ground, if a feeble but friendly state is in danger of being robbed of its independence and its sovereignty by a misuse of the name and power of the United States, the United States can not fail to vindicate its honor and its sense of justice by an earnest effort to make all possible reparation.

These principles apply to the present case with irresistible force when the special conditions of the Queen's surrender of her sovereignty are recalled. She surrendered not to the provisional government, but to the United States. She surrendered not absolutely and permanently, but temporarily and conditionally until such time as the facts could be considered by the United States. Furthermore, the provisional government acquiesced in her surrender in that manner and on those terms, not only by tacit consent, but through the positive acts of some members of that government who urged her peaceable submission, not merely to avoid bloodshed, but because she could place implicit reliance upon the justice of the United States, and that the whole subject would be finally considered at Washington.

I have not, however, overlooked an incident of this unfortunate affair which remains to be mentioned. The members of the provisional government and their supporters, through not entitled to extreme sympathy, have been led to their present predicament of revolt against the Government of the Queen by the indefensible encouragement and assistance of our diplomatic representative. This fact may entitle them to claim that in our effort to rectify the wrong committed some regard should be had for their safety. This sentiment is strongly seconded by my anxiety to do nothing which would invite either harsh retaliation on the part of the Queen or violence and bloodshed in any quarter. In the belief that the Queen, as well as her enemies, would be willing to adopt such a course as would meet these conditions, and in view of the fact that both the Queen and the provisional government had at one time apparently acquiesced in a reference of the entire case to the United States Government, and considering the further fact that in any event the provisional government by its own declared limitation was only "to exist until terms of union with the United States of America have been negotiated and agreed upon," I hoped that after the assurance to the members of that government that such union could not be consummated I might compass a peaceful adjustment of the difficulty.

Actuated by these desires and purposes, and not unmindful of the inherent perplexities of the situation nor of the limitations upon my power, I instructed Minister Willis to advise the Queen and her supporters of my desire to aid in the restoration of the status existing before the lawless landing of the United States forces at Honolulu on the 16th of January last, if such restoration could be effected upon terms providing for clemency as well as justice to all parties concerned. The conditions suggested, as the instructions show, contemplate a general amnesty to those concerned in setting up the provisional government and a recognition of all its *bona fide* acts and obligations. In short, they require that the past should be buried, and that the restored Government should reassume its authority as if its continuity had not been interrupted. These conditions have not proved acceptable to the Queen, and though she has been informed that they will be insisted upon, and that, unless acceded to, the efforts of the President to aid in the restoration of her Government will cease, I have not thus far learned that she is willing to yield them her acquiescence. The check which my plans have thus encountered has prevented their presentation to the members of the provisional government, while unfortunate public misrepresentations of the situation and exaggerated statements of the sentiments of our people have obviously injured the prospects of successful Executive mediation.

I therefore submit this communication with its accompanying exhibits, embracing Mr. Blount's report, the evidence and statements taken by him at Honolulu, the instructions given to both Mr. Blount and Minister Willis, and correspondence connected with the affair in hand.

In commending this subject to the extended powers and wide discretion of the Congress, I desire to add the assurance that I shall be much gratified to cooperate in any legislative plan which may be devised for the solution of the problem before us which is consistent with American honor, integrity, and morality.

GROVER CLEVELAND.

EXECUTIVE MANSION, *Washington, December 18, 1893.*

Partially as a consequence of the Spanish-American War and the intense lobbying of the Republic of Hawaii, President William McKinley eventually signed a joint resolution (Newlands Resolution), which provided for the annexation of Hawaii, on July 7, 1898. Hawaii later was admitted to statehood on August 21, 1959.

Despite the long history of U.S. involvement with the Hawaiian Islands and the enactment of federal programs for the benefit of Native Hawaiians under the plenary power vested in Congress in Article I, section 8, clause 3 of the United States Constitution, an official apology to Native Hawaiians on behalf of the United States for the overthrow of the Kingdom of Hawaii, with the participation of citizens and agents of the United States, has never been extended, nor has there ever been an attempt by the United States to develop a federal policy addressing their rights.

LEGISLATIVE HISTORY

S.J. Res. 19 was introduced by Senator Akaka for himself and Senator Inouye on January 21, 1993, and was referred to the Committee on Indian Affairs. This legislation is identical to S.J. Res. 335, a resolution which unanimously passed the Senate on October 7, 1992. S.J. Res. 335 did not reach the House Floor before the adjournment of the 102nd Congress.

COMMITTEE RECOMMENDATION AND TABULATION OF VOTE

On January 29, 1993, the Committee on Indian Affairs, in an open business session, considered S.J. Res. 19 and the resolution was ordered reported without an amendment by a majority vote of a quorum present, with a recommendation that the bill be passed by the Senate.

SECTION-BY-SECTION ANALYSIS

The whereas clauses of S.J. Res. 19 detail the history of events leading up to the January 17, 1893 overthrow and Hawaii's subsequent 1898 annexation and 1959 admission to statehood.

Section 1 provides that the Congress acknowledges the historical significance of the overthrow of the Kingdom of Hawaii on January 17, 1893, and apologizes to Native Hawaiians on behalf of the United States for the overthrow of the Kingdom of Hawaii on January 17, 1893, with the participation of agents and citizens of the United States, and the deprivation of the rights of Native Hawaiians to self-determination.

Section 2 provides a definition for the term "Native Hawaiians".

Section 3 provides that nothing in the joint resolution is intended to serve as a settlement of any claims against the United States.

REGULATORY IMPACT STATEMENT

Paragraph 11(b) of rule XXVI of the Standing Rules of the Senate requires each report accompanying a resolution to evaluate the regulatory and paperwork impact that would be incurred in carrying out this resolution. The Committee believes that S.J. Res. 19 will have no regulatory or paperwork impact.

EXECUTIVE COMMUNICATIONS

The Committee received no executive communications at the time of markup.

CHANGES IN EXISTING LAW

In compliance with subsection 12 of rule XXVI of the Standing Rules of the Senate, the Committee states that enactment of S.J. Res. 19 will not result in any changes in existing law.

○

Resolved by the Senate and the House of Representatives of the United States of America in Congress assembled,

SECTION 1. ACKNOWLEDGEMENT AND APOLOGY.

The Congress–

(1) on the occasion of the 100th anniversary of the illegal overthrow of the Kingdom of Hawaii on January 17, 1893, acknowledges the historical significance of this event which resulted in the suppression of the inherent sovereignty of the Native Hawaiian people;

(2) recognizes and commends efforts of reconciliation initiated by the State of Hawaii and the United Church of Christ with Native Hawaiians;

(3) apologizes to Native Hawaiians on behalf of the people of the United States for the overthrow of the Kingdom of Hawaii on January 17, 1893 with the participation of agents and citizens of the United States, and the deprivation of the rights of Native Hawaiians to self-determination;

(4) expresses its commitment to acknowledge the ramifications of the overthrow of the Kingdom of Hawaii, in order to provide a proper foundation for reconciliation efforts between the United States and the Native Hawaiian people; and

(5) urges the President of the United States to also acknowledge the ramifications of the overthrow of the Kingdom of Hawaii and to support reconciliation efforts between the United States and the Native Hawaiian people.

SECTION 2. DEFINITIONS.

As used in this Joint Resolution, the term "Native Hawaiian" means any individual who is a descendent of the aboriginal people who, prior to 1778, occupied and exercised sovereignty in the area that now constitutes the State of Hawaii.

SECTION 3. DISCLAIMER.

Nothing in this Joint Resolution is intended to serve as a settlement of any claims against the United States.

Approved November 23, 1993.

/s/ William Clinton

Kaʻimi Pono Press is publishing other materials about the history, culture and natural environment of these precious Hawaiian islands. Non-profit groups and educational organizations should write to us about bulk purchase discounts for your members or for fund-raising efforts. Send requests to: Special Sales Dept., Kaʻimi Pono Press, 91-216 Holoimua Place, Kapolei, HI 96707.